TRAILBLAZERS
of the
MODERN WORLD

THURGOOD MARSHALL

By Geoffrey M. Horn

WORLD ALMANAC® LIBRARY

Please visit our web site at: www.worldalmanaclibrary.com
For a free color catalog describing World Almanac® Library's list
of high-quality books and multimedia programs, call 1-800-848-2928 (USA)
or 1-800-387-3178 (Canada). World Almanac® Library's fax: (414) 332-3567.

Library of Congress Cataloging-in-Publication Data

Horn, Geoffrey M.
    Thurgood Marshall / by Geoffrey M. Horn.
        p. cm. — (Trailblazers of the modern world)
    Includes bibliographical references and index.
    Summary: An introduction to the life and accomplishments of the African American civil rights attorney
who became a prominent Supreme Court justice.
    ISBN 0-8368-5098-X (lib. bdg.)
    ISBN 0-8368-5258-3 (softcover)
    1. Marshall, Thurgood, 1908-1993—Juvenile literature. 2. United States. Supreme Court—Biography—
Juvenile literature. 3. African American lawyers—Biography—Juvenile literature. 4. African American
judges—Biography—Juvenile literature. [1. Marshall, Thurgood, 1908-1993. 2. Lawyers. 3. Judges.
4. United States. Supreme Court—Biography. 5. African Americans—Biography.] I. Title. II. Series.
    KF8745.M34H67 2004
    347.73'2634—dc22
    [B]   2003065364

First published in 2004 by
World Almanac® Library
330 West Olive Street, Suite 100
Milwaukee, WI 53212 USA

Copyright © 2004 by World Almanac® Library.

Project manager: Jonny Brown
Editor: Alan Wachtel
Design and page production: Scott M. Krall
Photo research: Diane Laska-Swanke
Indexer: Walter Kronenberg

Photo credits: © AP/Wide World Photos: 4, 8, 34 top, 39; © Terry Ashe/Time Life Pictures/Getty Images: 42;
© Bettmann/CORBIS: cover, 14, 15, 20, 23, 31, 32 top, 35 bottom; © CORBIS: 5, 11 top, 13, 18, 19 bottom,
22, 27, 37, 41; © Alfred Eisenstaedt/Time Life Pictures/Getty Images: 19 top; Courtesy of Langston Hughes
Memorial Library, Lincoln University Archives, Pennsylvania: 17; © Hulton Archive: 6 both, 11 bottom, 16,
21, 24, 25, 29; © Carl Iwasaki/Time Life Pictures/Getty Images: 30; © Cynthia Johnson/Time Life Pictures/Getty
Images: 26; © Wally McNamee/CORBIS: 9; © Francis Miller/Time Life Pictures/Getty Images: 34 bottom; © Flip
Schulke/CORBIS: 35 top; Photographer Unknown, Collection of the Supreme Court of the United States: 10;
© Time Life Pictures/Getty Images: 32 bottom

Printed in the United States of America

1 2 3 4 5 6 7 8 9 08 07 06 05 04

TABLE of CONTENTS

Words that appear in the glossary are printed in **boldface**
type the first time they occur in the text.

CHAPTER 1

BEATING JIM CROW

When Thurgood Marshall was born in 1908, most black Americans were living in the shadow of Jim Crow. The purpose of the Jim Crow laws was to make sure that blacks had less education, political power, and economic opportunity than whites.

Marshall dedicated his whole life to beating **Jim Crow**. To a remarkable extent, he succeeded—first as a lawyer for the National Association for the Advancement of Colored People (NAACP), next as a federal judge, then as a top official at the United States Department of Justice, and finally as a justice of the United States Supreme Court. The fact that Jim Crow laws no longer exist is due in large part to the work of Marshall and his NAACP legal team.

Standing outside the U.S. Supreme Court, Marshall (center) and two legal colleagues enjoyed their moment of triumph after the Court outlawed school segregation on May 17, 1954.

ORIGINS OF JIM CROW

More than nine million African Americans were living in the United States at the time of Marshall's birth. Over 80 percent of them lived in the eleven southern states that had been part of the **Confederacy**—the states that had fought against the Union during the **Civil War**. In 1861, when the Civil War began, nearly all the blacks in these states

How Jim Crow Got Its Name

The term "Jim Crow" dates from the 1820s, when a song-and-dance man named Thomas "Daddy" Rice copied a number he heard from a black man whose name happened to be Jim Crow. Rice, who was white, blackened his face with burnt cork or charcoal paste, dressed himself up to look like Crow, and became nationally famous for his crude and clownish "blackface" act.

Many other white entertainers did their own blackface versions of the "Jim Crow" character. By the end of the nineteenth century, the name was broadly applied both to the racist stereotype and to the racist laws that degraded black people.

Pictures like this one were part of "Jim Crow"—the racist stereotypes and unjust laws that discriminated against African Americans.

were slaves. In 1863, while the Civil War was raging, President Abraham Lincoln issued the Emancipation Proclamation, freeing many of the slaves in the rebellious southern states. In 1865, after the Union had won the war, the Thirteenth Amendment to the United States Constitution became the law of the land. The Thirteenth Amendment made slavery illegal throughout the nation.

After the Civil War, the freed slaves tried to exercise their basic rights, but southern whites—who feared the freed blacks' political and economic power—were determined to stop them. The southern whites passed laws known as the Black Codes. These racist laws varied from state to state, but they usually limited the kinds of jobs blacks could hold, barred them from meeting in groups after sunset, and made it illegal for them to buy or carry a gun. Any African-American found "idle" in public might be sentenced to up to a year of hard labor. The aim of the Black Codes was to deny blacks their

The Black Codes tried to limit freed blacks to the kinds of jobs they performed as slaves, such as picking cotton.

This lynching took place in Texas in 1907, just one year before Marshall was born.

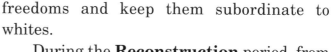

freedoms and keep them subordinate to whites.

During the **Reconstruction** period, from 1865 to 1877, the United States government stepped in to defend the rights of blacks. The Black Codes were declared illegal, and many African Americans began to vote and run for public office. By the end of 1877, however, the federal government had lost interest in protecting the freed slaves. Whites in the South struck back hard, using several powerful weapons to reverse the gains that blacks had made.

One weapon was terror, some of it carried out by the **Ku Klux Klan**. Nearly 5,000 African Americans were hanged, shot, burned, or **mutilated** by white lynch mobs between 1880 and 1950. In Maryland, where Marshall grew up, at least eighteen African Americans were lynched. The last known lynching in Maryland took place in 1933, the same year Marshall graduated from law school.

A second weapon was the law. Even as some whites were breaking the law by threatening and lynching blacks, others were passing new laws that forced African Americans to ride in separate rail cars and attend separate schools. Nearly all states in the South banned marriages between whites and blacks and made it as difficult as possible for African Americans to vote.

States bordering on the South also took steps to impose racial **segregation**. In Marshall's home state of Maryland, a law passed in 1884 imposed prison sentences of from eighteen months to ten years on blacks and whites who married. A minister convicted of performing an interracial marriage could be forced to pay a fine of $100. As late as 1955, the state passed a law that any white woman who gave birth to a child fathered by a black man could be sentenced to up to five years in prison. The United States Supreme Court overturned all legal barriers to intermarriage in 1967, just before Marshall joined the Court.

In His Own Words—Thurgood Marshall on Jim Crow

In 1978, while serving on the Supreme Court, Marshall issued an opinion in which he described how Jim Crow laws had spread to the North as well as the South. He also pointed out that after Woodrow Wilson became president in 1913, segregation of the races was an official policy of the United States government.

The segregation of the races was extended in residential areas, parks, hospitals, theaters, waiting rooms, and bathrooms. There were even [laws] which authorized separate phone booths for Negroes and whites, which required that textbooks used by children of one race be kept separate from those used by the other, and which required that Negro and white prostitutes be kept in separate districts. . . .

Nor were the laws restricting the rights of Negroes limited solely to the Southern States. In many of the Northern States, the Negro was denied the right to vote, prevented from serving on juries, and excluded from theaters, restaurants, hotels, and inns. Under President Wilson, the Federal Government began to require segregation in Government buildings; desks of Negro employees were curtained off; separate bathrooms and separate tables in the cafeterias were provided; and even the galleries of the Congress were segregated.

WORKING WITHIN THE SYSTEM

Like many Americans, both black and white, Marshall knew that the Jim Crow laws were unfair and unjust. He and his colleagues at the NAACP filed paper after paper, lawsuit after lawsuit, until, slowly but steadily, the walls of segregation crumbled. This work was diffi-

Marshall, the first black Supreme Court justice, was honored on a stamp issued by the U.S. Postal Service in January 2003.

cult and dangerous. Marshall received many threats from racists. On at least one occasion, he came close to being lynched.

One of Marshall's early legal victories came in 1935, when he convinced a Maryland state court to require the University of Maryland law school to end its ban on admitting African American students. His greatest courtroom triumph came nineteen years later in *Brown v. Board of Education*. In that landmark case, Marshall persuaded the U.S. Supreme Court to rule that racially segregated public schools violated the Constitution. In all, as chief lawyer for the NAACP, he won twenty-nine out of the thirty-two cases he argued before the U.S. Supreme Court.

Unrivaled as a lawyer, renowned as a storyteller, and popular as a public speaker, Marshall was the nation's best-known civil rights leader in the 1940s and 1950s. In 1961, President John F. Kennedy chose him to become the first African American on the United States Court of Appeals for the Second Circuit, one of the nation's highest courts. To honor him, the courthouse in downtown New York City where the Second Circuit judges meet was renamed the Thurgood Marshall United States Courthouse in 2003.

In 1965, President Lyndon B. Johnson selected Marshall to fill one of the top posts at the Justice Department: **solicitor general** of the United States. Two years later, Johnson singled him out for an even higher honor. The president nominated Marshall to become a justice on the Supreme Court. When he was confirmed, Marshall became the first African American to serve in the nation's highest court.

WEAKNESSES AND STRENGTHS

Although Marshall is a much-admired figure, he was no saint. He partied more than he studied in his younger years, and he was not a faithful husband to his first wife, who died in 1955. During the 1960s, he quarreled openly with some younger black leaders. By the time he announced his retirement from the Court in 1991, the elderly Marshall was barely on speaking terms with some of the other justices.

One Supreme Court justice who remained his friend and admirer was Sandra Day O'Connor. O'Connor, the first woman to serve on the Supreme Court, saw Marshall, the first black justice, as a pioneer like herself. In 1992, a year before his death, O'Connor wrote this tribute to Marshall in the *Stanford Law Review*:

Associate Justice Sandra Day O'Connor, the first woman on the Supreme Court, is one of Marshall's great admirers.

> *His was the eye of a lawyer who saw the deepest wounds in the social fabric and used the law to heal them. His was the ear of a counselor who understood the vulnerabilities of the accused and established safeguards for their protection. His was the mouth of a man who knew the anguish of the silenced and gave them a voice. . . . No one could avoid being touched by his soul.*

CHAPTER 2

"WAY UP SOUTH"

Thurgood Marshall was born July 2, 1908, in the northwestern part of Baltimore, Maryland, where his family had an apartment on McMechen Street. Although, strictly speaking, Maryland is not a southern state, Marshall always considered himself a southerner. He was born "way up South," he told an interviewer in 1977.

Marshall as a baby, when he was known as Thoroughgood or "Goody."

FAMILY BACKGROUND

Thurgood's father, William ("Willie") Canfield Marshall, was a proud but difficult man who drank too much. He worked as a dining car waiter and sleeping car porter on a railroad when his children were young. Later, he was a steward at the Gibson Island Club, on Chesapeake Bay, where Thurgood also worked during his college days. Willie, who was of mixed-race

Through with "Thoroughgood"

On his birth certificate, Marshall's first name is actually spelled "Thoroughgood." This was a tribute both to his uncle, also named Thoroughgood Marshall, and to his paternal grandfather, Thorney Good Marshall. Twelve years old when the Civil War broke out, Thorney Good is said to have escaped from slavery on Virginia's eastern shore and settled in Baltimore as a free man.

The younger Thoroughgood knew the storied history of his complicated name, but would have none of it. "By the time I was in second grade," he told a reporter, "I got tired of spelling all that and shortened it."

background, with light skin and blue eyes, was in charge of hiring and supervising the country club's all-black dining room staff. The country club catered to Maryland's white elite; no African-Americans or Jews could be members.

Thurgood's mother, Norma Arica Williams, worked as a schoolteacher. Unlike Willie, who was a school dropout, Norma grew up in a family that prized education. Her father, Isaiah Williams, had sailed to South America with the United States Navy, had developed a love for opera and Shakespeare, and ran a thriving grocery business in Baltimore. Her mother, Mary Fossett, was a teacher in a black private school. The name "Norma" came from a famous nineteenth-century Italian opera, and the name "Arica" came from the city, now part of Chile, where Isaiah first heard the opera sung. Marshall adored his mother, who was fiercely loyal to her children. "Her only fault," he recalled, "was that if she was with you, if you were in the family, she was with you, right or wrong."

Norma was nineteen years old and Willie was twenty-two when they fell in love. She was enrolled in a teacher-training program at what is now Coppin State College in Baltimore when she became pregnant. They married in April 1905, she finished her studies, and in September they had their first child, William Aubrey Marshall. Aubrey, Thurgood's older brother, studied medicine and dentistry and became a doctor. Willie and Norma expected Thurgood also to study dentistry. But Thurgood had other ideas.

When Marshall was growing up, Baltimore officials tried to keep well-to-do areas like Mount Vernon Place off-limits to blacks.

Marshall's father Willie worked as a waiter in a dining car like this one.

In His Own Words—Thurgood Marshall on Growing Up in Baltimore

In 1910, the Baltimore city council passed a law setting strict boundaries to separate the city's white and black neighborhoods. Decades later, Marshall described in detail what it was like to grow up "way up South," in a segregated city.

A study was made by the Urban League around 1930 which showed that segregation in Baltimore was more rigid than any other city in the country, including Jackson, Mississippi. I know this is almost unbelievable, but it's true. In the department stores downtown, a Negro was not allowed to buy anything off the counters. As you went in the store, you were told to get the hell out.

Another thing I remember very well was that there were no toilet facilities available to Negroes in the downtown area, and I remember one day, I had to go, and the only thing I could do was get on a trolley car and try to get home. And I did get almost in the house, when I ruined the front doorsteps. That gives you an idea what we went through.

FIGHTING WORDS

Measured by the standards of black families at the time, or even of many black families today, Willie and Norma Marshall were by no means poor. When Willie was unemployed, however, the Marshall family faced financial hardship. During one of the tougher times, in 1910, Norma's older sister Denmedia invited the young family to leave Baltimore and move to Harlem, in New York City. Her husband, Clarence Dodson, had a job with the New York Central Railroad, and the Dodsons felt sure that Willie could also find work there. For the next four years, while Willie and Clarence waited on dining car passengers, Norma and Denmedia took care of the two boys in the Dodsons' Lenox Avenue apartment. Thurgood, nicknamed "Goody," was a beautiful child, eager to please.

That changed after 1914, when the Marshalls had to return to Baltimore because Norma's mother had broken her leg. This time, Norma's older brother Fearless Williams and his wife Florence opened their doors to the Marshall family. "Uncle Fee" and "Aunt Flo" shared their house on Division Street with the four Marshalls until 1920, when Willie and Norma were able to get a home of their own.

Thurgood was enrolled in a segregated school on Division Street that had a reputation as the best "colored elementary school" in the city. Although he remembered his teachers as "better than average," he did not make life easy for them. When he acted up, which was often, he would have to sit in the first seat of the first row, so his teachers could keep a close eye on him. His classmates did not think of the young Thurgood as much of a fighter, although he remembered his father encouraging him "to lay some knuckles on any white man who called [you] a nigger."

This historic photo of an all-black school, taken by the social reformer Lewis Hine, dates from the period when Marshall was attending a "colored elementary school" in Baltimore.

When he was only seven years old, Thurgood began doing odd jobs for a Jewish merchant named Hale, who ran a neighborhood grocery store. Hale, who paid Thurgood ten cents a day to deliver groceries, had a son named Sammy, who soon became Thurgood's closest friend. Hale had taught his son not to fight back when taunted, but Thurgood disagreed. "We used to have fights, fusses, because he would let people call him a 'kike' and wouldn't fight back," Marshall said later. "If anybody called me 'nigger,' I fought 'em."

CHAPTER 3

LESSONS IN LIFE AND LAW

Like the Marshall family, many Americans were fascinated by the real-life dramas that unfolded daily in the nation's courtrooms. The most famous court case of the 1920s was the so-called "Monkey Trial," in which lawyer Clarence Darrow (right) challenged a Tennessee law that banned the teaching of evolution in the public schools.

Marshall graduated in the top third of his class at Baltimore's Colored High School, but he was hardly an outstanding student. Still, if you look carefully at his early life, you can see glimmerings of the lawyer he would become.

One of his father's favorite pastimes was to drop by the local courthouse and stand in the back of a courtroom as the lawyers argued a case. Then he would head home to try out the lawyers' arguments and strategies on his sons. When Marshall was asked, after he had joined the Supreme Court, how he had first become interested in the law, he pointed to those family arguments four or five decades earlier.

Now you want to know how I got involved in law? I don't know. The nearest I can get is that my dad, my brother, and I had the most violent arguments you ever heard about anything. I guess we argued five out of seven nights at the dinner table. When we were away at college, and we would come back, the first dinner we'd have—I remember a neighbor of ours, Mrs. Hall, would tell her husband, "Ah, the boys are home."

The reason was, she could hear the arguments through the walls.

Something else for which those family arguments prepared Marshall was a starring role on the high school debate team. It's likely that another of his other notable high school achievements—memorizing the entire Constitution—also helped him succeed as a debater. It was punishment for misbehaving, however, not love for the law, that originally led Thurgood to memorize the Constitution!

THE WRONG SIDE OF THE LAW

When he was fifteen years old, Marshall had a serious encounter with the way the law treated blacks in the 1920s. One day, while working for a hat maker named Mortimer Schoen, the gangly adolescent pushed his way onto a trolley with an armload of four boxed hats. "Nigger, you just stepped in front of a white woman," said an angry white man, pulling him off the streetcar. The hat boxes dropped to the ground, fists flew, a crowd gathered, and within minutes—and without asking any questions—a policeman hauled Thurgood off to jail. The hat maker put up $50 to bail him out.

"I'm really sorry I busted up four of your hats," Marshall told his boss.

"Did the man really call you a nigger?" Schoen asked him.

"Yes, sir, he sure did," Marshall replied. Schoen told Thurgood he had done the right thing. He never asked the young man to pay for the hats or pay back the $50.

Another episode of Thurgood's youth that could have turned into more than just a brush with the law occurred while he was working Sundays for a bootlegger—a man who sold illegal liquor. "His name was 'Smoothie,'" Marshall told an interviewer many years later.

As a teenager, Thurgood worked for a bootlegger named "Smoothie." Bootleggers used many tricks to smuggle liquor, including hiding the bottles in what looked like a lumber truck.

Like Marshall, the writer Langston Hughes attended Lincoln University of Pennsylvania in the 1920s. This photo shows Hughes in 1945, when he was one of the nation's best-known poets.

"That's all I remember. In my late teens, my father used to take me to Smoothie's operation on an island just outside Baltimore. We'd take a motor launch, climb onto a pier, and face a bunch of guys with machine guns and rifles. Boy, was I impressed!"

Thousands of dollars in cash would change hands during an afternoon of high-stakes illegal gambling. Why didn't the police ever raid the place? "With all the machine guns out there, who was gonna raid 'em?" Besides, said Marshall, "They were paying off somebody."

COLLEGE YEARS

After graduating from high school, Marshall worked for the Baltimore & Ohio Railroad for six months in order to raise money for college. In September 1925, he enrolled at Lincoln University in Pennsylvania, the same mostly black college his brother had attended. Another student at Lincoln during the late 1920s was Langston Hughes, already a published poet. Hughes was not impressed by the younger man, describing him as "rough and ready, loud and wrong, good natured and uncouth."

Marshall reveled in fraternity life, with its crude hazing and rude pranks. He rarely studied, relying on his quick mind to get good grades. He was tall and well muscled, and his handsome face now sported a mous-

tache. He was attractive to women—and he knew it.

After numerous engagements—the total number is rumored to be at least nine—he married Vivian "Buster" Burey, an eighteen-year-old student at the University of Pennsylvania, while he was in his final year at Lincoln. Later, he spoke frankly about what had attracted him to Buster. "She wasn't beautiful. No way all that beautiful. But she was put together nicely—black hair, black eyes, and very nice. She got along with me."

At least one member of his mother's family was not very hopeful about his prospects. Fearless Williams—"Uncle Fee"—warned Buster and her parents that his nephew Thurgood "always was a bum, is a bum, and always will be a bum." But Buster would not be put off. She and Thurgood were married in 1929, at the First African Baptist Church in Philadelphia.

In his freshman year at Lincoln University, Thurgood (second row, second from right) joined an elite African-American fraternity, Alpha Phi Alpha.

FINDING HIS MISSION

Whatever Uncle Fee thought, Buster believed in Thurgood, and so did his mother. When her son declared, after graduating with honors from Lincoln in January 1930, that he wanted to go to law school, Norma Marshall was determined to make it happen.

The easiest solution would have been for him to enroll at the law school of the University of Maryland in Baltimore. It had a fine reputation, low tuition, and a good location, not far from the Marshalls' home. There was only one problem: the school did not admit blacks and had no interest in changing its policy.

Since Marshall could not afford to attend a good northern law school that admitted blacks, his only

The writer Zora Neale Hurston ranks, with Marshall, among Howard's most famous students.

Howard University

Established in 1867, Howard University was originally intended as a training school for black ministers. Even before it opened, however, it had taken on a broader purpose as a "University for the education of youth in the liberal arts and sciences and other departments." Although Howard's main mission has always been to educate African-Americans, its charter has never put any restrictions on the race or sex of the students who go there.

Howard University is named for Oliver Otis Howard (1830–1909), who was the university's president from 1869 to 1874. Howard, a white man who grew up in Maine, was both a professional soldier and a committed Christian. He commanded troops on the Union side in some of the major battles of the Civil War. After the war he was put in charge of the Bureau of Refugees, Freedmen, and Abandoned Lands. This federal government agency, better known as the Freedmen's Bureau, was responsible for providing emergency aid, distributing land, and setting up schools for the freed slaves.

Famous Howard students and teachers include, in addition to Marshall, the authors Zora Neale Hurston and Toni Morrison, Nobel Peace Prize winner Ralph Bunche, former UN Ambassador Andrew Young, and opera diva Jessye Norman.

practical option was Howard University, which welcomed African Americans. His savings were not enough to pay for tuition at Howard, but his mother would not let that stop him. Norma pawned her engagement and wedding rings so that her son could attend Howard's law school.

In the late 1920s, Howard's law school did not have a good reputation. Its program was not **accredited**, and the entire faculty was part-time. The school was known as a "dummy's retreat" because many of its students would have had a hard time getting admitted anywhere else. In 1930, however, the law school named a new chief administrator, Charles Hamilton Houston. Almost single-handedly, Houston turned the school into the nation's most important training ground for black lawyers.

Houston's own academic record was beyond challenge. As a student at Harvard University, he had been the first African-American to become an editor of the influential *Harvard Law Review*. He had gone on to earn a doctoral degree at Harvard and had studied law in Spain, at the University of Madrid. Since 1924, he had practiced law in Washington, D.C., and he had been a member of the Howard law school faculty.

Houston had two main goals. The first was to make Howard a

The Howard University campus as it looked in the 1940s.

Howard University's law library, photographed around 1900.

fully accredited law school with a full-time faculty. The second was to produce top-quality attorneys who would use the power of the law to fight Jim Crow and make life better for black people. Houston succeeded brilliantly in achieving both goals. His teaching changed Thurgood Marshall's life forever, giving Marshall a mission he never forgot.

In His Own Words—Thurgood Marshall on Charles Houston

Born in 1895, Charles Hamilton Houston died of a heart attack in 1950. Marshall was a Supreme Court justice in the late 1970s when he delivered this generous tribute to the great Howard University professor.

A man of vision. A big man. Strong. He loved people. If he came to visit you, when he got back to Washington you got a letter thanking you and asking "How are you doing?"—and your wife, calling her by name; and your children, calling them by name, and your dog, calling him by name. Because he loved life. And he loved people. . . .

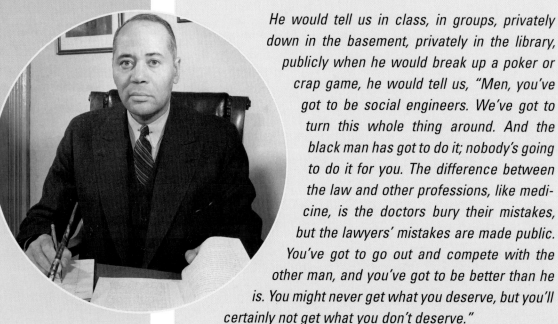

Charles Houston in 1939

He would tell us in class, in groups, privately down in the basement, privately in the library, publicly when he would break up a poker or crap game, he would tell us, "Men, you've got to be social engineers. We've got to turn this whole thing around. And the black man has got to do it; nobody's going to do it for you. The difference between the law and other professions, like medicine, is the doctors bury their mistakes, but the lawyers' mistakes are made public. You've got to go out and compete with the other man, and you've got to be better than he is. You might never get what you deserve, but you'll certainly not get what you don't deserve."

CHAPTER 4

BREAKING DOWN BARRIERS

Serious at long last about his studies, Marshall graduated first in his class from Howard University law school in 1933. After passing the state bar exam, which allowed him to practice law in the state of Maryland, Marshall opened a tiny law office in Baltimore. Much of his work involved routine matters like divorce, debt collection, and real estate.

Times were tough. The United States was in the middle of a terrible economic depression, and over 40 percent of Baltimore's black community was on welfare. As a beginning lawyer, Marshall found it difficult to attract clients, especially clients who could pay. "He had a genius for ignoring cases that might earn him any money," said a secretary who worked for him back then. To keep his office afloat, Marshall had to take on a part-time job as a file clerk at a Baltimore health clinic.

Many African Americans lost their jobs and their homes during the economic depression of the 1930s.

FIRST VICTORY—THE MURRAY CASE

Despite his money problems, Marshall did not forget the lessons that Charles Houston had taught him. Nor did he forget the hurt he had suffered in 1930, when the University of Maryland law school had refused to admit him because of his African ancestry.

Marshall was eager to challenge the university's Jim Crow policy, and in 1935 he got his chance. Houston let him know about Donald Murray—a graduate, like Houston, of Amherst College—who had been turned down by the University of Maryland law school. Marshall took Murray's case and, with careful coaching by Houston, won a decision from a trial judge in June that forced the school to let Murray in.

Even after Murray began taking classes at the university, school officials appealed to a higher court to reverse the trial judge's decision. The university admitted that Maryland had only one state-supported law school, which enrolled whites but completely excluded blacks. The university argued that the state had fulfilled its duty to black students by offering a scholarship fund to help them attend law schools outside the state. (In fact, the entire fund was only $600—

Marshall, Donald Murray, and Charles Houston (left to right) sued the University of Maryland in a 1935 case that brought Thurgood his first major legal victory over segregation.

very little for this purpose, even in 1933.) The appeals court was not impressed. In upholding the trial judge's decision, the court ruled that if the state university provided a law school education for whites, it would need to do the same for African Americans.

COUNSEL FOR THE NAACP

In 1935, while Murray's case was working its way through the courts, Charles Houston left the faculty of Howard University law school to become full-time special **counsel** for the National Association for the Advancement of Colored People (NAACP). The NAACP was the leading organization dedicated to winning equal rights for African Americans as citizens of the United States. It was founded in New York City on February 12, 1909—less than a year after Marshall was born. The choice of date for its founding—Abraham Lincoln's birthday—was no coincidence. Lincoln was honored by African Americans and their white allies as "the Great Emancipator," the president who had done more than anyone else to free the slaves.

A more immediate reason for founding the organization on Lincoln's birthday was that, in August 1908, a white mob had rampaged through Springfield, Illinois, where Lincoln had spent much of his life. The mob destroyed the black business district, burned down houses in a poor black neighborhood, and lynched two black men. Four whites also lost their lives in the riot, and more than forty black

The NAACP published the first issue of its monthly magazine, *The Crisis*, in 1910.

"Lynch's Law"

In addition to working to stamp out Jim Crow, the NAACP campaigned to end lynchings. Lynchings were acts of mob violence in which people were put to death without a trial. Most lynchings took place in the old Confederacy, but they also occurred in states bordering on the South.

In all likelihood, the word "lynching" comes from Charles Lynch, an eighteenth-century Virginia planter. Lynch and his fellow officers became well known in the early 1780s for dealing out rough punishments to suspected lawbreakers, without a jury trial or a sentence from a judge. By the mid-nineteenth century, "Lynch's Law" was a well-known term throughout the United States and Britain.

To publicize its campaign against lynching, the NAACP displayed this flag at its New York City headquarters in the late 1930s.

families were left homeless. If all this could happen in the city of Lincoln, where in the United States could any African American feel safe?

As special counsel for the NAACP, Houston saw an opportunity to put into practice a plan he had been developing for years. Instead of trying to strike down Jim Crow all at once, he proposed bringing a series of more specific cases that would be easier to win. His strategy called for NAACP lawyers to challenge segregation in school after school, state after state, just as he and Marshall had begun to do in Maryland. That way, when the NAACP legal team launched a lawsuit that would end Jim Crow once and for all, there would already be a settled body of legal decisions in their favor.

Marshall also saw an opportunity. His law practice was floundering, and he was desperate for money. "Things are getting worse and worse," he wrote Houston in May 1936. He was already spending a great deal of his time on unpaid work for the NAACP. "Personally, I would not give up these cases here in Maryland for the world," he continued, "but at the same time there is no opportunity to get down to really hustling for business." He asked for a **retainer** from the NAACP of $150 a month.

Houston had the solution to both their problems. He recommended that Thurgood and Buster move to New York City, where the NAACP had its national office. Thurgood would become a full-time member of the legal department at a monthly salary of $200. This was not a huge sum of money for someone of Marshall's abilities and education. But it was a lot more than he was making in Baltimore—and it was the work he wanted to be doing.

The NAACP stood in the front lines against racial injustice in 1945, helping black soldiers who faced discrimination when they came home from World War II.

"MR. CIVIL RIGHTS"

By the end of the 1930s, Houston had given up his NAACP post and resumed his law practice in Washington, D.C. With Houston's departure, Marshall became chief counsel for the newly formed NAACP Legal Defense and Educational Fund, with the challenge of making Houston's hopes come true. During the 1940s and 1950s, Marshall traveled throughout the

The NAACP Today

Now approaching its 100th birthday, the NAACP is the nation's oldest civil rights group. The organization went through a rough period in the early 1990s, when feuds and scandals tarnished its image. Since then, however, the NAACP has rebounded. Today, the organization has about 500,000 members, with 1,700 local branches in the 50 states plus 120 chapters on college and university campuses.

The NAACP today has its national headquarters in Baltimore and maintains an office in Washington, D.C. Kweisi Mfume, a former member of Congress, has been NAACP president since 1996.

United States, working on cases, delivering speeches, meeting with local NAACP officials, and raising money for the fund. Eventually, he became so well known that he was nicknamed "Mr. Civil Rights."

Marshall received many death threats during this period. He was almost lynched in November 1946, while an NAACP legal team was in Columbia, Tennessee, defending two black men charged with attempted murder. As a mob of angry whites gathered near the black business district, Marshall and the other lawyers decided they needed to make a quick escape. They drove hurriedly toward Nashville, while the mob chased a decoy car in the opposite direction. When the mob finally caught up with the decoy, said Marshall, "They beat the driver bad enough that he was in the hospital for a week."

A longtime opponent of segregation, former First Lady Eleanor Roosevelt joined the NAACP board of directors in the mid-1940s. Marshall is seated next to her at right.

In His Own Words—Dangerous Work

Dozens of people lost their lives in the struggle for equal rights. As Marshall traveled from town to town in the Deep South, he survived many dangerous situations. He was very brave—but also very lucky. In the following passage, Marshall reflects on a terrifying experience he had while changing trains in Hernando, Mississippi.

I had about a two- or three-hour stopover. And while I was waiting I got hungry, and I saw a restaurant. So I decided that if I got hungry enough I'd go over there and put my civil rights in my back pocket and go to the back door of the kitchen and see if I could buy a sandwich. . . . This white man came up beside me in plain clothes with a great big pistol in a case on his hip and he said, "Nigger, boy, what are you doing here?" And I said, "Well, I'm waiting." And he said, "What did you say?"

I said, "Sir, I'm waiting for the train to Louisiana—Shreveport." And he said, "Well, there's only one train comes through here and that's the four o'clock. You better be on it, because the sun is never going down on a live nigger in this town." And you know what? I wasn't hungry anymore. It dawned on me that he could just blow my head off and he wouldn't even have to go to court."

CHAPTER 5

THE "BROWN" REVOLUTION

The Supreme Court's decision in *Brown v. Board of Education* (1954) marked the greatest triumph in the history of the NAACP and the high point of Thurgood Marshall's career. But the road to *Brown* was paved with many smaller victories, all of them important for the NAACP's legal strategy.

Case Names

Most legal cases that Marshall dealt with came to the courts as a result of a dispute. The name of a case—for example, *Brown v. Board of Education*—shows the names of the people or organizations involved in the dispute. The "v." in the middle stands for versus, a Latin word that means "against."

CHALLENGING "SEPARATE BUT EQUAL"

The legal foundation of Jim Crow was a decision in 1896 by the United States Supreme Court. This decision, known as *Plessy v. Ferguson*, had upheld a Louisiana law requiring railroads to provide "equal but separate accommodations for the white and colored races." The law also allowed police to arrest any African American found riding in a car reserved for whites. For decades, whenever Jim Crow laws were challenged, state and local officials had pointed to the "separate but equal" standard embraced by the Court. If Marshall was going to end Jim Crow, he would need to chip away at the "separate but equal" doctrine.

The first step was to show that "separate but equal" often really meant separate and *unequal*. The NAACP had its first big Supreme Court victory in 1938 in a case involving a student named Lloyd Gaines. Gaines, who was president of his senior class at Lincoln University in Missouri, applied to the whites-only law school at the University of Missouri. School officials there turned him down but said that if he applied to Lincoln—which had no law school—then Lincoln would immediately create one. Since a separate, spur-of-the-moment law school at Lincoln was obviously unequal to the established legal education program at the University of Missouri, the Supreme Court ruled in Gaines's favor.

During the Jim Crow era, many African Americans in the segregated South had little choice but to shop in "colored only" stores like this one.

The next step for Marshall was to show that, by their very nature, segregated schools were *always* unequal. He argued that they were always unequal because they made black students feel unworthy and inferior to whites. Because they were always unequal, said Marshall, they violated the Fourteenth Amendment to the United States Constitution. The Supreme Court accepted this reasoning in two cases in 1950, the same year that Charles Houston, Marshall's great teacher, died of a heart attack.

In *McLaurin v. Oklahoma State Regents*, the Court ruled that the University of Oklahoma had violated the United States Constitution when it forced a black graduate student to sit in a separate row in class, work at a separate desk in the library, and eat at a sepa-

The Fourteenth Amendment

Added to the Constitution shortly after the Civil War, the Fourteenth Amendment defined for the first time what it meant to be a citizen of the United States. It declared that anyone born in the United States was an American citizen, regardless of whether that person had been born free or as a slave.

One part of the Fourteenth Amendment says that no state may deny to any person "the equal protection of the laws." This part, known as the **Equal Protection Clause**, means that state or local governments may not discriminate against anyone on the basis of race, sex, religion, ethnic group, or national origin.

rate table in the school cafeteria. The Court said that an African American student admitted to a formerly all-white state university had to be treated exactly the same as all other students.

In *Sweatt v. Painter*, a second case decided on the same day, the Court held that a segregated law school opened for Texas blacks could never be equal to the well-established, whites-only law school the University of Texas already had. The only remedy, said the Court, was

The Brown case took its name from Linda Brown (front), who was required by the city of Topeka, Kansas, to attend a segregated elementary school in the early 1950s.

In His Own Words—The Impact of Segregated Schools

In an article published in 1952 in the *Journal of Negro Education*, Marshall explained why he believed it was so important to outlaw racial segregation in the public schools.

Although no social scientist can say that segregated schools alone give the Negro feelings of insecurity, self-hate, undermine his ego, make him feel inferior and warp his outlook on life, yet for the child the school provides the most important contact with organized society. What he learns, feels, and how he is affected there is apt to determine the type of adult he will become. Social scientists have found that children at a very early age are affected by and react to discrimination and prejudice. . . .

The elimination of segregation in public schools may not remove all of the causes of insecurity, self-hate, etc., among Negroes, but since this is a state-sponsored program, certainly the state . . . should not be a party to a system which does help produce these results. This is the thesis which is now being used to demonstrate the unconstitutionality of segregation at the public elementary and high school levels.

for the University of Texas law school to admit African Americans on an equal basis with whites.

LANDMARK DECISION

The NAACP strategy was working. Both the *McLaurin* and *Sweatt* cases had been decided by **unanimous** vote. Even before the *Brown* case was argued, the nine Supreme Court justices had agreed privately among themselves that segregation was bound to fall.

Three important questions remained. First, when would the decision come? Second, would the decision be unanimous? And, third, when the Court decided that school segregation violated the Constitution, how quickly would states with segregated school systems be required to change?

Although the full name of the case that outlawed Jim Crow was *Brown v. Board of Education of Topeka, Kansas*, it involved far more than one city or one state. Bundled into the *Brown* case were separate lawsuits from the states of Kansas, South Carolina, Virginia, and Delaware. All these lawsuits made the claim that segregation of the public schools violated the Constitution and harmed black children. When he argued the case before the Supreme Court, Marshall came armed with research by Dr. Kenneth Clark showing that segregated schools were harmful to black children's self-image and self-esteem.

In 1954, the Supreme Court spoke with one voice when it ruled that school segregation was unlawful. The unanimous opinion, delivered for

Dr. Kenneth Clark did the research that allowed Marshall to prove to the Supreme Court that segregated schools were harmful to black children.

Chief Justice Earl Warren delivered the Supreme Court's unanimous opinion in the Brown case.

Marshall's landmark Supreme Court victories earned him a place on the cover of *Time* magazine in 1955.

the Court by Chief Justice Earl Warren, overturned *Plessy v. Ferguson* and concluded that "in the field of public education the doctrine of 'separate but equal' has no place."

The Court waited another year before sharing its judgment on the third question: When would states need to integrate their school systems? The answer, offered in 1955, was with "all deliberate speed." The meaning of this phrase was left unclear. It probably didn't mean "right now," but it certainly didn't mean "a hundred years from now." What it did mean was that, for the next two decades, the nation would be in turmoil, as Marshall and the NAACP pushed the courts to enforce the law of the land, and many southern states did everything in their power to resist the necessary changes.

OVERCOMING RESISTANCE

For Marshall, victory in the *Brown* case had a bitter-sweet aftertaste. Notably absent from the NAACP victory party after the Supreme Court announced its decision on May 17, 1954, was Thurgood's wife Buster. Their marriage had been far from perfect. While campaigning for equal rights, he had been away from home for days, even weeks at a time. Those who knew him well were sure he had not always been faithful to Buster during those long nights on the road. Thurgood and Buster had wanted to have children, but her pregnancies had ended in **miscarriages**. More recently, her health had begun to fail. She rarely felt like going out. During this period, Thurgood had been spending more and more time in the company of an NAACP staffer, Cecelia ("Cissy") Suyat.

Around November 1954, Thurgood learned that his wife had lung cancer. Taking time off from work, he remained by her bedside for the next three months, as her condition worsened. Finally, on February 11, 1955, at the age of forty-four, Vivian "Buster" Marshall passed away.

After Thurgood got over his grief from Buster's death, he asked Cissy to marry him. She hesitated at first, fearing that Thurgood's marriage to a "foreigner"—she had been born in Hawaii, to Filipino parents—might provide fuel for scandal. Thurgood overcame her concerns, however, and on December 17 they were married at St. Philip's Episcopal Church in Harlem. She and Thurgood had two sons: Thurgood Jr. ("Goody"), born in 1956, and John, born two years later.

In 1967, when he became a Supreme Court justice, Marshall's family included his wife Cissy and their two sons, Thurgood Jr. and John (front).

The Arkansas National Guard stopped black students from entering Little Rock's Central High School in 1957 until the federal government intervened.

The late 1950s posed new challenges for Marshall. The *Brown* decision had wounded Jim Crow, but it had not dealt the death blow for which the NAACP had hoped. In some southern states, white officials launched a program of "massive resistance." They chose to shut down their entire public school systems rather than allow black children to enter formerly all-white schools. Marshall and other NAACP lawyers faced howling mobs as they went from courthouse to schoolhouse, working to make sure local officials obeyed the courts and allowed black children to attend school with whites.

Marshall also had problems with members of the African-American community, some of whom thought he was too willing to compromise with whites. Younger black leaders, including Martin Luther King Jr., agreed with Marshall that the Jim Crow laws needed to be overturned. But these younger leaders were impatient with the courts, which could take months or years to reach a decision. Instead, the younger leaders favored tactics such as boycotts, protest marches, and sit-ins. Marshall was troubled by these tactics, because they sometimes involved breaking the law. On the other hand, he greatly admired King, and he came up with a successful legal strategy to defend the sit-ins. He also recognized that by violating unjust laws and braving the anger and violence of racists, the protesters were winning worldwide sympathy and support for the African-American cause.

One of Marshall's fiercest critics among the younger black leaders was a fiery orator named Malcolm X, who thought blacks should give up trying to integrate with whites and develop separate political, economic, and cultural organizations. Malcolm and his militant followers called Marshall a "fool" who was working "hand in glove with the white folks." Marshall was not persuaded by their criticisms. "Malcolm X and I never got along," he said later, "because I just don't believe that everything that's black is right, and everything that's white is wrong."

Marshall feared that militant blacks were tarnishing the image of the entire civil rights movement. To preserve the reputation of the NAACP, he met secretly with J. Edgar Hoover, the director of the Federal Bureau of Investigation, and began feeding information to the FBI. Historians now

know that Hoover was no friend of the civil rights movement and that he conducted a vicious smear campaign against King. At the time, however, Marshall was doing what he thought best to preserve the progress that African Americans had made under NAACP leadership.

In His Own Words—Thurgood Marshall on Lawyers

These remarks, delivered while Marshall was serving as solicitor general, were published in the *Washington University Law Quarterly* in 1967.

*The lawyer has often been seen by minorities, including the poor, as part of the **oppressors** in society. Landlords, loan sharks, businessmen specializing in shady installment credit schemes—all are represented by counsel on a fairly permanent basis. But who represents and speaks for tenants, borrowers, and consumers? Many special interest groups have permanent associations with retained counsel who seek and sponsor advantageous legislation. But who represents and speaks for the substantial segment of the populace that such legislation might disadvantage? Outside of the political processes, I think the answer is clear. Lawyers have a duty in addition to that of representing their clients; they have a duty to represent the public, to be social reformers in however small a way.*

MOVING ON AND MOVING UP

By the end of the 1950s, Marshall was becoming weary of his battles with both the segregationists and the militants. He was worn down by the struggle he had led for more than two decades. He knew it was time to move on.

He spent some of 1960 overseas, helping to write a constitution for Kenya, an African country that became fully independent three years later. In September 1961, President John F. Kennedy nominated Marshall to become a federal judge on the United States Court of Appeals for the Second Circuit, which deals with cases in New York, Connecticut, and Vermont. The nomination ran into trouble in the United States Senate—which, under the Constitution, had the power to accept or reject the president's choice. Finally, after twelve months of wrangling, the Senate approved Marshall. Southern Democrats cast all the votes against him.

In 1965, President Lyndon B. Johnson summoned Marshall to Washington to become solicitor general of the United States. In that job, one of his main responsibilities was to argue cases before the Supreme Court. As solicitor general, Marshall appeared before the Court nineteen times and won fifteen of the cases he argued.

Johnson wanted to make history by naming Marshall as the first black justice of the Supreme Court. He could not do this, however, until a vacancy on the Court opened up. The president, who was accustomed to getting what he wanted, found a unique way to create an open seat. He appointed Ramsey Clark, the son of Supreme Court Justice Tom C. Clark, to head the Department of Justice as attorney general. His son's new job put the elder Clark in an awkward position, since the Supreme Court frequently had to deal with the

Meeting at the White House with President Lyndon B. Johnson, Marshall called his wife from the Oval Office to tell her that Johnson planned to name him to the Supreme Court.

Justice Department, and the father-son bond between the two Clarks created an obvious **conflict of interest**.

Tom Clark had little choice but to step down from the Court, giving Johnson the vacancy he needed. Clark resigned on June 12, 1967. The following day, Johnson named Marshall to replace him. The Senate confirmed Marshall as a Supreme Court justice in late August by a margin of 69–11.

Times were changing. The Court's senior associate justice was Hugo Black, a native of Alabama. In his younger days, Black had been a member of the Ku Klux Klan. Now, this white son of the South—who, over time, had become a friend of Marshall's—had the honor of giving the oath of office to the Court's first African-American member.

LBJ

Lyndon Baines Johnson—also known by his initials LBJ—was one of the most complex and tragic figures ever to hold the presidency. LBJ, who became president after John F. Kennedy was killed in 1963, saw his own presidency crumble five years later because of an unpopular war in Vietnam.

Although he was a white man who grew up in the segregated South, LBJ did more than any president since Lincoln to advance the cause of civil rights. In addition to placing Marshall on the Supreme Court, he pushed through the Civil Rights Act of 1964; got Congress to pass the Voting Rights Act of 1965; and appointed the cabinet's first African-American member in 1966.

CHAPTER 7

MR. JUSTICE MARSHALL

When he joined the Supreme Court in the fall of 1967, "Mr. Civil Rights" became "Mr. Justice Marshall." Since the mid-1950s, under the leadership of Chief Justice Earl Warren, the Court had been a force for racial justice and social change. Marshall expected to contribute in a major way to the Warren Court's era of accomplishment. What he could not have known in 1967 was that the Warren Court era was just about over.

An official portrait of the Supreme Court in November 1990. Seated in the center is Chief Justice William Rehnquist; the other justices include Marshall (seated, second from right) and O'Connor (standing, second from left).

FRUSTRATIONS ON THE COURT

The Court began to change in 1969, when Earl Warren retired. President Richard M. Nixon chose Warren Burger of Minnesota as the new chief justice. Burger believed that in many

Change of Address

When Marshall took his seat on the Supreme Court, all the justices were men, so it was considered proper to address any justice of the Court as "Mr."—for example, "Mr. Justice Marshall." In 1981, however, when the Court got its first woman member, the correct form of address became simply "Justice Marshall" or "Your Honor."

In His Own Words—Thurgood Marshall on Racial Justice

One of the most important cases Marshall faced during his time on the Court was *Regents of the University of California v. Bakke* (1978). The Bakke case involved affirmative action—the idea that special efforts must be made to help members of minority groups that have been the victims of prejudice. In *Bakke*, the Court had to decide whether a medical school violated the Constitution when it set up a special admissions program that could be filled only by members of minority groups. The Court ruled that the university could consider race when selecting students but could not set up any kind of rigid system of racial quotas.

Marshall thought the Court did not go far enough in supporting the idea of affirmative action. In this discussion of the *Bakke* case, written in the late 1970s, he argued that African Americans as a group still carried the scars of centuries of ill treatment.

The position of the Negro today in America is the tragic but inevitable consequence of centuries of unequal treatment. Measured by any benchmark of comfort or achievement, meaningful equality remains a distant dream for the Negro. . . .

When the Negro child reaches working age, he finds that America offers him significantly less than it offers his white counterpart. For Negro adults, the unemployment rate is twice that of whites, and the unemployment rate for Negro teenagers is nearly three times that of white teenagers. . . . Although Negroes represent 11.5% of the population, they are only 1.2% of the lawyers and judges, 2% of the physicians, 2.3% of the dentists, 1.1% of the engineers and 2.6% of the college and university professors.

The relationship between those figures and the history of unequal treatment afforded to the Negro cannot be denied. At every point from birth to death, the impact of the past is reflected in the still disfavored position of the Negro.

In light of the sorry history of discrimination and its devastating impact on the lives of Negroes, bringing the Negro into the mainstream of American life should be a state interest of the highest order. To fail to do so is to ensure that America will forever remain a divided society.

areas of the law the Court had moved too far, too fast. As chief justice, he did not reverse the landmark rulings of the previous decade, but he slowed the pace of change. Burger took himself very seriously—a trait that Marshall would sometimes poke fun at by greeting the chief justice with a hearty "What's shakin', chiefy baby?"

During his twenty-four years as an associate justice, Marshall was the Court's most consistent voice for the victims of poverty, bigotry, and abuse of power. He was also an unshakable foe of the death penalty, arguing that the way capital punishment was imposed in the United States would "cast a pall over our society for years to come." In the case of *Roe v. Wade*, Marshall was among the seven justices who decided to legalize abortion.

Marshall was aware that with each passing year his views were shared by fewer and fewer of his fellow justices. One by one, the justices who had ruled so boldly in *Brown* and later cases departed from the Court. It was especially discouraging for Marshall when his closest friend and ally among the justices, William J. Brennan Jr., announced his retirement in 1990.

The Supreme Court became much more cautious after President Richard M. Nixon (right) chose Warren Burger (left) to replace the retiring Earl Warren as chief justice in 1969.

"HE DID THE BEST HE COULD"

By 1991, as he approached his eighty-third birthday, Marshall's health was failing and his mood had grown sour. On June 27, in a letter to President George H. W. Bush, he wrote that because of his "advancing age and medical condition" he planned to retire from the Court as soon as a new associate justice could be confirmed. At a press conference after the letter was made public, a reporter asked him if he could be more specific about his medical problems.

"What's wrong with you, sir?" the reporter continued.

"What's wrong with me?" said Marshall. "I'm old and coming apart!"

To replace Marshall on the Court, President Bush chose Clarence Thomas. Some people in the civil rights movement were cheered that Bush had chosen another African American for the Court. Others felt Thomas's skin color could not hide that he had little sympathy for civil rights or other issues that concerned most black Americans. Marshall kept a discreet public silence, but he let friends of his know he took a dim view of his replacement.

In the twilight of his career, an ailing Marshall told a 1991 press conference that he was leaving the Supreme Court.

Marshall lived less than two years after he stepped down from the Court. He died at the Bethesda Naval Hospital in Maryland on January 24, 1993.

Many wonderfully complimentary things were said about him after his passing. Associate Justice Lewis F. Powell Jr., who served with Marshall, said he thought

Marshall "did more to establish equal justice under the law" than Martin Luther King Jr. or anyone else. "No American," said Powell, "did more to lead our country out of the wilderness of segregation than Thurgood Marshall."

Marshall himself summed up his career more modestly. When asked by a reporter how he would like to be remembered, the former civil rights leader and Supreme Court justice answered, "He did the best he could with what he had."

In His Own Words—Thurgood Marshall on Uniting the Nation

On July 4, 1992, at Independence Hall in Philadelphia, Marshall received the Philadelphia Liberty Medal, which carried with it a cash award of $100,000. The ceremony for the award was one of his last public appearances, and he spoke with passion about the need for Americans to overcome divisions of race and class.

The legal system can force open doors and, sometimes, even knock down walls. But it cannot build bridges. That job belongs to you and me. We can run from each other, but we cannot escape each other. We will only attain freedom if we learn to appreciate what is different and muster the courage to discover what is fundamentally the same. Take a chance, won't you? Knock down the fences that divide. Tear apart the walls that imprison. Reach out; freedom lies just on the other side.

TIMELINE

1908	Thoroughgood (later Thurgood) Marshall is born July 2, in Baltimore, Maryland.
1909	National Association for the Advancement of Colored People (NAACP) is founded February 12.
1929	Marshall marries Vivian "Buster" Burey.
1930	Graduates with honors from Lincoln University, Pennsylvania.
1933	Receives law degree from Howard University, graduating first in his class. Opens a private law practice.
1935	Wins *Murray* case, forcing the University of Maryland law school to admit its first black student.
1936	Hired as a staff lawyer for the NAACP. Moves with Buster to New York City.
1954	In Marshall's biggest case, *Brown v. Board of Education*, the U.S. Supreme Court overturns school segregation.
1955	Buster dies of lung cancer February 11. Marshall marries Cecelia "Cissy" Suyat December 17.
1961	President John F. Kennedy nominates Marshall for a federal judgeship on the U.S. Court of Appeals for the Second Circuit.
1965	President Lyndon B. Johnson names Marshall solicitor general of the United States.
1967	Ramsey Clark becomes U.S. attorney general. His father, Tom C. Clark, resigns from the Supreme Court. Marshall is named to fill Clark's seat, becoming the first African American on the Court.
1969	Warren Burger replaces Earl Warren as chief justice of the Supreme Court.
1990	Marshall's closest friend on the Court, William J. Brennan Jr., retires.
1991	Marshall announces his retirement from the Court on June 27.
1993	Dies January 24 in Bethesda Naval Hospital, Maryland.

accredited: officially approved by professional groups.

Civil War: the war (1861–1865) between the Union (northern states) and the Confederacy (southern states). Slavery in the southern states was a major cause of the conflict, which was won by the Union.

Confederacy: the group of eleven southern states that withdrew from the Union in 1860 and 1861.

conflict of interest: a clash between one's personal motives and public duty.

counsel: a lawyer.

Equal Protection Clause: the part of the Fourteenth Amendment that requires state governments to provide equal legal protection for all.

Jim Crow: racist laws and practices intended to make sure that blacks had less education, political power, and economic opportunity than whites.

Ku Klux Klan: a secret society that favors white supremacy and has used threats and violence to intimidate black Americans.

miscarriages: pregnancies that, for unplanned medical reasons, fail to result in the birth of a baby.

mutilated: severely injured or crippled, often by having had a limb cut off or destroyed.

oppressors: people who use their authority in unjust ways to keep other people powerless and poor.

Reconstruction: the period (1865–1877) after the Civil War when the states of the Confederacy were under the direct control of the federal government before being readmitted to the Union.

retainer: money paid to a lawyer in advance, in exchange for legal services.

segregation: separation of the races, enforced by law.

solicitor general: a high-ranking official in the Department of Justice who argues cases before the Supreme Court.

unanimous: without disagreement.

TO FIND OUT MORE

BOOKS

Aldred, Lisa. *Thurgood Marshall (Black Americans of Achievement)*. New York: Chelsea House, 1990.

Anderson, Wayne. *Brown v. Board of Education: The Case Against School Segregation*. New York: Rosen, 2003.

Bullard, Sara. *Free at Last: A History of the Civil Rights Movement and Those Who Died in the Struggle*. New York: Oxford University Press, 1993.

Compston, Christine L. *Earl Warren: Justice for All*. New York: Oxford University Press, 2002.

Patrick, John J. *The Young Oxford Companion to the Supreme Court of the United States (Oxford Student Companions to American Government)*. New York: Oxford University Press, 1994.

Tushnet, Mark V. (ed.). *Thurgood Marshall: His Speeches, Writings, Arguments, Opinions, and Reminiscences*. Chicago, Ill.: Lawrence Hill Books, 2001.

INTERNET SITES

African-American Odyssey: The Civil Rights Era
http://memory.loc.gov/ammem/aaohtml/ exhibit/aopart9.html
Library of Congress documents show how the civil rights era affected politics, culture, and sports.

Brown v. Board of Education
http://www.landmarkcases.org/brown/ home.html
The civil rights case that gave Marshall his greatest legal triumph.

Brown v. Board of Education National Historic Site
http://www.nps.gov/brvb/
Dedicated to the site in Topeka, Kansas, where the landmark case began.

History of Jim Crow
http://www.jimcrowhistory.org/home.htm
Story of segregation in the American South.

NAACP
http://www.naacp.org/
Official site of the National Association for the Advancement of Colored People.

Oyez: U.S. Supreme Court Multimedia
http://www.oyez.org/oyez/tour/
Offers a virtual tour of the Supreme Court.

About the Author

Geoffrey M. Horn is a freelance writer and editor with a lifelong interest in politics and the arts. He is the author of books for young people and adults, and has contributed hundreds of articles to encyclopedias and other reference books, including *The World Almanac*. He graduated summa cum laude with a bachelor's degree in English literature from Columbia University, in New York City, and holds a master's degree with honors from St. John's College, Cambridge, England. He lives in southwestern Virginia, in the foothills of the Blue Ridge Mountains, with his wife, four cats (at last count), and one rambunctious collie. This book is dedicated the memory of Louis and Estelle Horn and Robert and Luise Davidson.